DISCOVER 🐾 DOGS WITH THE AMERICAN CANINE ASSOCIATION

AMERICAN CANINE ASSOCIATION, INC.

ACA

America's Largest Veterinary Health Tracking Canine Registry

OFFICIAL SEAL ®

♥ • ♥ • ♥ • ♥ I LIKE ♥ • ♥ • ♥ • ♥

GERMAN SHEPHERDS!

Linda Bozzo

It is the Mission of the American Canine Association (ACA) to provide registered dog owners with the educational support needed for raising, training, showing, and breeding the healthiest pets expected by responsible pet owners throughout the world. Through our activities and services, we encourage and support the dog world in order to promote best-known husbandry standards as well as to ensure that the voice and needs of our customers are quickly and properly addressed.

Our continued support, commitment, and direction are guided by our customers, including veterinary, legal, and legislative advisors. ACA aims to provide the most efficient, cooperative, and courteous service to our customers and strives to set the standard for education and problem solving for all who depend on our services.

For more information, please visit www.acacanines.com, e-mail customerservice@acadogs.com, phone 1-800-651-8332, or write to the American Canine Association at PO Box 121107, Clermont, FL 34712.

Enslow Elementary, an imprint of Enslow Publishers, Inc.

Enslow Elementary® is a registered trademark of Enslow Publishers, Inc.

Library of Congress Cataloging-in-Publication Data

Bozzo, Linda.
  I like German shepherds! / Linda Bozzo.
    p. cm. — (Discover dogs with the american canine association)
  Includes bibliographical references and index.
  Summary: "Early readers will learn how to care for a German shepherd, including breed-specific traits and needs"—Provided by publisher.
  ISBN 978-0-7660-3849-3
  1. German shepherd dog—Juvenile literature. I. Title.
  SF429.G37B69 2012
  636.737'6—dc22
                                    2011010476

Future editions:
Paperback ISBN 978-1-4644-0119-0
ePUB ISBN 978-1-4645-1026-7
PDF ISBN 978-1-4646-1026-4

Printed in China

012012 Leo Paper Group, Heshan City, Guangdong, China

10 9 8 7 6 5 4 3 2 1

To Our Readers: We have done our best to make sure all Internet Addresses in this book were active and appropriate when we went to press. However, the author and the publisher have no control over and assume no liability for the material available on those Internet sites or on other Web sites they may link to. Any comments or suggestions can be sent by e-mail to comments@enslow.com or to the address on the back cover.

Every effort has been made to locate all copyright holders of material used in this book. If any errors or omissions have occurred, corrections will be made in future editions of this book.

Photo Credits: Angelika Fischer/Photos.com, p. 13 (hamburger); Anna Idestam-Almquist/Photos.com, p. 23; Annette Shaff/Photos.com, p. 13 (collar); Claudia Steininger/Photos.com, p. 10; Daniel Bendjy/Photos.com, p. 6; Emmanuelle Bonzami/Photos.com, p. 11; Eric Isselée/Photos.com, p. 3 (left); Everett Collection, p. 17; © iStockphoto.com/Marilyn Nieves, p. 19; © iStockphoto.com/webphotographeer, p. 18; Jason Lugo/Photos.com, p. 3 (right); jclegg/Photos.com, p. 13 (leash and rope); Nikolai Tsvetkov/Photos.com, pp. 1, 22; Shutterstock.com, pp. 5, 9, 13 (German shepherd, bed, brush, bowls), 21; © Steve Lomas, p. 14.

Cover Photo: Eric Isselée/Photos.com (German shepherd puppy).

Enslow Elementary
an imprint of
Enslow Publishers, Inc.
40 Industrial Road
Box 398
Berkeley Heights, NJ 07922
USA
http://www.enslow.com

CONTENTS

IS A GERMAN SHEPHERD RIGHT FOR YOU?

German shepherds are best for families who have a lot of energy. These dogs are very smart and like to keep busy.

German shepherds make good guard dogs because they like to keep their families safe. They need to get used to strangers and other pets while they are still puppies.

German shepherds
are loyal
and strong.

Puppies need more attention than older dogs.

A DOG OR PUPPY?

Puppies are cute and fun, but training them takes time. German shepherds need to be trained at an early age.

Does your family have time to play with and train a puppy? For some families, an older dog that is already trained is better.

German shepherds grow to be large dogs. The males are bigger than the females.

LOVING YOUR GERMAN SHEPHERD

German shepherds are not happy just lying around the house. They need to be kept busy with games and exercise.

German shepherds are often used as working dogs. They work as search and rescue dogs, police dogs, and guide dogs. They enjoy having jobs. And they love being loved!

Many search and
rescue dogs are
German shepherds.

German shepherds come in other colors besides tan and black.

EXERCISE

German shepherds enjoy playing fetch.
They should also be taken on long walks
on a **leash** every day to help tire them out.

German shepherds have lots of energy!

FEEDING YOUR GERMAN SHEPHERD

German shepherds can be fed wet or dry dog food. Ask the **veterinarian (vet)**, a doctor for animals, which food is best for your dog and how much to feed her. Dogs need fresh, clean water every day.

Remember to keep your dog's food and water dishes clean. Dirty dishes can make her sick.

Do not give your dog people food. It can make her sick.

Your new dog will need:

a collar with a tag

a bed

a brush

food and water dishes

a leash

toys

GROOMING

German shepherds **shed** a lot. This means their hair falls out. They need to be brushed at least once a week, sometimes more.

Bathe your dog as often as you need to. Use a gentle soap made just for dogs.

You also need to clip your dog's nails. A vet or **groomer** can show you how.

WHAT YOU SHOULD KNOW

German shepherds need to exercise their bodies and their minds. If they get bored, they can get in trouble by chewing on things.

German shepherds are also easy to train. They make good watchdogs because they are brave.

FUN FACT:
Rin Tin Tin was a famous German shepherd that starred in movies and on television.

A movie poster for The Return of Rin Tin Tin.

You will need to take your new dog to the vet for a checkup. He will need shots, called vaccinations, and yearly checkups to keep him healthy. If you think your dog may be sick or hurt, call your vet.

A GOOD FRIEND

Your dog will be a good friend to you for a long time. German shepherds can live up to thirteen years or longer. Love and care for your dog, and he will be a great pet!

NOTE TO PARENTS

It is important to consider having your dog spayed or neutered when the dog is young. Spaying and neutering are operations that prevent unwanted puppies and can help improve the overall health of your dog.

It is also a good idea to microchip your dog, in case he or she gets lost. A vet will implant a microchip under the skin that contains your contact information, which can then be scanned at a vet's office or animal shelter.

Some towns require licenses for dogs, so be sure to check with your town clerk.

For more information, speak with a vet.

There are many dogs, young and old, waiting to be adopted from animal shelters and rescue groups.

groomer—A person who cuts a dog's fur and nails.

leash—A chain or strap that connects to a dog's collar.

shed—When a dog's hair falls out so new hair can grow.

vaccination—A shot that dogs need to stay healthy.

veterinarian (vet)—A doctor for animals.

Read About Dogs

Books

Beal, Abigail. *I Love My German Shepherd.* New York: PowerKids Press, 2011.

Rajczak, Kristen. *German Shepherds.* New York: Gareth Stevens Publishing, 2011.

Internet Addresses

American Canine Association: Kids Corner
<http://acakids.com/>

Janet Wall's How to Love Your Dog: The German Shepherd
<http://loveyourdog.com/gsd.html>

INDEX